No Words

Collected and adapted by Jin Rou Shi for the
Buddist Text Translation Society
Illustrated by Tara and Cintya Kandahsari
Book Design by Sue Ellen Parkinson
Composition by Crista Goddard

Published by:
Buddhist Text Translation Society
4951 Bodhi Way
Ukiah
CA 95482 USA

First edition 2008
10 09 08 07 06 05 04 03 02   10 9 8 7 6 5 4 3 2 1

ISBN 978-088139-426-9

Printed in Malaysia

Addresses of the Dharma Realm Buddhist
Association's branch
offices are listed at the back of this book.

— No Words —
Teachings of the Buddha

The Deer King

A long time ago, in the royal park of Benares, the Buddha appeared as a king of deer named Banyan Deer King. His coat was golden like the sun and his horns glistened like silver. He watched over a herd of five hundred deer. Not far away, another herd of five hundred deer was led by another golden deer named Branch. In the tall grass and shadows of the forest, the two herds lived together in peace.

One day the Prince of Benares was out on a hunt and spied the deer. "What a perfect hunting ground!" he cried, and into the park he dashed with his hunters. When he saw Banyan Deer King and Branch Deer, he withdrew his bow. "Shoot all the deer you want," he told his hunters. "But spare the golden ones."

Thereafter, he came to the park every day and killed more deer than was needed for his dinner table. At sight of the hunters, the deer would dash off, yet many were killed and wounded by the flying arrows.

Banyan Deer King called the herds together and said, "Friends, we know there is no escape from death, but this needless killing must be stopped. Let the deer draw lots to be killed, one a day from each herd."

The next day Banyan Deer King and Branch Deer paid the prince a visit and discussed their plan with him. "Very well," said the prince, admiring the wisdom of the deer kings. "Send a deer tomorrow."

The first lot fell to a pregnant doe from Branch Deer's herd. She begged him, "Grant that I be passed over until after my fawn is born. Then I will gladly take my turn."

"No one wants to take your place," Branch Deer said. "You must go."

In despair, the poor doe went to Banyan Deer King and explained her plight. He said, "Go in peace. I shall put your turn upon another." Then he went to the palace and laid his golden head upon the chopping block. A deep silence fell upon the forest.

When the prince saw Banyan Deer King ready for sacrifice, he said, "You're the leader of the herd. You should be the last to die."

Banyan Deer King said, "I came to save the life of a doe whose fawn is yet to be born."

The prince's eyes filled with tears. "Among men and beasts, I have never known such compassion. Arise, Banyan Deer King, I spare your life and the life of the doe."

Banyan Deer King did not move. "So we shall be free? But what about the other deer and furry animals? And the birds and the fish, what will they do?"

"I shall also spare their lives," said the prince. "All creatures of the land, sea, and sky will be free." Banyan Deer King raised his head from the chopping block and returned to the forest.

Banyan Deer King did not move. "So we will be free? But what about the other deer and furry animals? And the birds and the fish, what will they do?"

1

The Buddha and the Mad Elephant

Devadatta, the Buddha's cousin, was jealous of the Buddha and wanted to kill him. One day, with a jug of whiskey, he went to the king's elephant stables in Rajagriha and said to the elephant keeper, "I will make you rich if you help me." And he told him of his wicked plan.

"So be it, sir," said the elephant keeper and emptied the jug of spirits into the trough of Nalagiri, the king's mighty elephant tusker. The next day he turned Nalagiri out down the road where the Buddha was walking. Loud trumpeting blasted the air. A cloud of dust rose up in front of the Buddha. Everyone yelled, "Run for your life. Nalagiri is loose."

Maddened with drink, Nalagiri lifted her trunk and charged the Buddha. Her eyes were red with fire and her tail was stretched out behind. Crowds of men, women, and children screamed wildly and scrambled to safety on the rooftops.

Raising his hand, the Buddha said, "Come, Nalagiri. Come, friend. Do not be mad and reckless. Do not harm anyone." From the tips of his fingers, like a ray of bright sunlight, the Buddha's loving-kindness streamed toward Nalagiri and embraced her.

She staggered and stopped, her huge ears fanning back and forth. Her eyes softened and two huge tears rolled down her old, wrinkled cheeks. Slowly, she knelt in front of the Buddha, her knees buckling under her. Stretching out her trunk, she cleaned the dust from his feet and blew it over her head.

"Come, I will take you home," said the Buddha, and he led her back to her stable. From then on, she was known as Nalagiri the Tame.

Unlike Nalagiri, Devadatta could not be tamed. Over the years, he became more evil and tried many ways to kill the Buddha. He hired some archers to shoot him. But they were so moved by the Buddha's loving-kindness that they dropped their bows when they saw him and became his disciples instead.

Later, Devadatta rolled a boulder off a cliff towards the Buddha. But before it crushed the Buddha, it broke into tiny pieces. A tiny piece cut the Buddha's foot causing it to bleed. For this act, Devadatta fell into the deepest hells. The Buddha took pity on him, saying, "After passing eons of time in hell, Devadatta will rise from the darkness and make good his evil ways. Then he will attain enlightenment as a Buddha called Heavenly King."

"Come, Nalagiri. Come, friend. Do not be mad and reckless. Do not harm anyone."

3

The Mustard Seed

Once upon a time in the city of Benares there lived a woman named Kisagotami, whose only son died. With the dead child in her arms, she ran from house to house, begging, "Please give me medicine for my son."

Upon seeing her, the people shook their heads in pity. "Poor Kisagotami, you have lost your senses. Your son is dead. He is beyond the help of medicine."

Kisagotami, however, refused to accept their words and went on wandering in the streets asking everyone she met for help. Finally, a gentle old man told her, "Go to the Buddha. He will help you."

In haste, Kisagotami carried her dead child to the Buddha and asked, "Is there a medicine to cure my son?"

The Buddha looked at the closed eyes of the child and understood. "I shall heal your son if you bring me a handful of mustard seed," he said. Joyfully, Kisagotami started off to get them. Then the Buddha added, "But the seed must come from a house where no one has died."

Kisagotami went to every house in the city, asking for the mustard seed. "We have plenty of mustard seed," everyone said. "Take all that you need."

Then Kisagotami asked, "Has anyone ever died in this house?"

"Of course," she was told. "There have been many deaths here."

"I lost my father and my sister," said one.

"I lost my daughter," said another. "There are more dead here than living." Kisagotami could not find a single house that had not been visited by death.

Weary and with all hope gone, she sat on a hilltop and watched the fires of the city flicker up and die out. Suddenly she came to her senses. "The lives of people flicker up and go out like fire," she said. "My son is not the only one who has died. Everyone dies. How selfish I am in my grief!"

She buried her son amid the wildflowers and returned to the Buddha. "Now I understand," she said, holding out an empty hand.

"I shall heal your son if you bring me a handful of mustard seed...But the seed must come from a house where no one has died."

The Littlest Lamp

Ages ago, in India, a poor old woman trudged off to the forest everyday to gather a bundle of firewood. When she had enough wood to sell, off to the market she went.

"Firewood! Firewood!" she cried. If all went well, she would earn enough for a handful of rice.

One day, on the road with her load, she met thousands of people carrying flowers and incense. They were dressed in their finest clothes and their faces were bright with joy.

"What is your hurry?" she asked.

"The Buddha has come to our village to teach us the Way to Happiness," a man said. "We're going to the temple to make offerings to him."

"I also wish to make an offering to the Buddha," the old woman said, and she hurried to the marketplace. "Firewood! Firewood!" she cried.

"I feel generous today," said a man of good heart. "I will pay you two coins for your wood."

The old woman danced with joy. With one coin, she bought a handful of rice to make her meal. With the other coin, she ran to the lamp shop. "One small lamp, please," she said to the shopkeeper.

Holding her little lamp, she rushed to the temple and quietly slipped through the temple door. For a moment, she was blinded by the glow of thousands of big, beautiful lamps that had been lit for the Buddha. Ashamed of her little lamp, she placed it at the back of the altar. Then she sat to the side and listened to the Buddha. Like a warm summer rain, his words of wisdom washed away her shame.

Suddenly a gust of wind came up and all the big, beautiful lamps were blown out. Only one little lamp was left burning. Its light was as bright as that of the thousand lamps. A monk asked, "Why is this little lamp still burning while the others blew out?"

The Buddha said, "This lamp was offered by a poor woman who gave her last coin. Because of her generosity, it will burn forever. And she will never again be poor."

For a moment, she was blinded by the glow of thousands of big, beautiful lamps that had been lit for the Buddha. Ashamed of her little lamp, she placed it at the back of the altar.

Sudanna

Once upon a time in India there was a youth named Sudanna who wanted to become enlightened. He set out on a journey looking for wise teachers. To the north, south, east and west, he went—through rain and snow, perils and dangers. No matter what, he never lost heart and was enchanted with all there was to learn.

His first journey took him to a small village in the north. There he met a doctor who taught him to care for the sick. From him, he learned compassion. He wanted to stay, but the doctor said, "Keep going south, on to your next teacher."

On the road, he met a poor old woman. "You must be hungry," she said and shared her only yam with him. From her, he learned giving. He would have followed her down the road, but she pointed to the seashore and said. "There is much to learn by the sea."

All along the seashore were hundreds of children building sand castles and listening to singing seashells. By watching them, Sudanna learned the simple joys of life. He would have stopped and played, but the children waved him on to the east. And from the east, he traveled to the west, following the course of the sun and moon.

In a marketplace, he overheard a rich merchant say to a friend, "If you wish to become wealthy, start by saving every small coin." From that, Sudanna learned that small acts add up to great acts.

At a temple, he saw a woman offering flowers to the Buddha. From her, he remembered to be thankful. "There is a monk in the forest," she said. "You will find him sitting under a sala tree."

Sudanna traveled on westward and found the kind-hearted monk who taught him to meditate. He learned that by having peaceful thoughts himself, he could bring peace to others.

Sudanna wanted to stay in the forest, but the monk urged him on to his next teacher. With tears in his eyes, he bowed to the monk and left for the countryside.

Farmers greeted Sudanna from across their fields. They quenched his thirst and gave him shelter in their barns. From them, Sudanna learned to be humble and content with whatever he had.

One day, while walking through the forest, Sudanna saw a tiny sprout growing out of a dead tree—a lesson in birth and death.

When daylight faded and night spread over the earth in the cool evenings, Sudanna slept underneath the trees and gazed at the moon in wonder. Then at the first glint of daylight, he was off again. In this manner, he continued along his journey, enthusiastically learning about life. Each lesson learned—a small enlightenment.

He learned that by having peaceful thoughts himself, he could bring peace to others.

Gold: A Poisonous Snake

One day the Buddha was walking down the road on his way to Benares. With him were three hundred disciples. Suddenly he stopped and pointed to a pot of gold barely visible in the grass by the road. "Look," he said. "A Poisonous Snake!"

A poor farmer, who was working in a field nearby, heard the Buddha and said, "I must go and protect the Buddha from the snake." But when he got to the road, the Buddha was out of sight. Looking around for the snake, the farmer saw, instead, the gold shining in the sunlight. "How lucky am I!" he cried and carried the gold home.

The next day the farmer saw a big cart for sale. "My cart is too small," he said. "I will buy a new one." Another day, he saw a strong, young ox for sale. "My ox is too old," he said. "I need a strong ox to pull my new cart." And the next day, he said, "My clothes are ragged," and he bought some fine new ones. And the next day and the next, he bought more and more things. "I need a big house," he said, and he had one built.

None of this went unnoticed by his neighbors. "Where did you get the gold?" they asked him.

"I found it on the road," he said.

They became jealous and told the king, who said, "The road belongs to me. The gold is mine and the farmer is a thief. He will be beheaded!"

The next morning the farmer was led to the Execution Square. The executioner lifted his shining sword over his head. The farmer, waiting for the final blow, sighed and said, "Now I know what the Buddha meant when he said that gold is a poisonous snake."

"Stop!" the king said to the executioner. "How do you know the Buddha?" he asked the farmer. And the farmer told him how he had heard the Buddha and found the treasure.

"The Buddha has great wisdom," said the king. "Because of gold, people become like poisonous snakes. How foolish of me to kill a man over gold."

So the King set the farmer free and returned the gold to him. In turn, the farmer gave it to the poor people in the village. Taking up the robes of a monk, he entered the forest. There he sat in blissful meditation contemplating his good fortune at having heard the wise teachings of the Buddha.

"The Buddha has great wisdom, ... Because of gold, people become like poisonous snakes..."

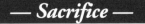
The Monkey King and the Mangos

Once upon a time the Buddha came into the world as a Monkey King and ruled over 80,000 monkeys. He was tall and strong and his wisdom shone like the sun. On the bank of the Ganges River, there grew a huge mango tree round like the moon. Every day the monkeys swung from branch to branch, chattering and eating the golden fruit that was big and sweet and delicious. One branch overhung the river. Sometimes a ripe mango fell from the branch into the water.

One day, while eating a mango, the Monkey King said, "Some day the fruit falling into the river will bring us danger. Strip the branch that overhangs the river," he told the little monkeys. "Leave not so much as a blossom.

But one mango, hidden by an ant's nest, was left unseen by the 80,000 monkeys. When it was large and ripe, it fell into the river and floated downstream where the King of Benares was bathing. The king picked up the mango and tasted it. "This is delicious!" he said. "I must have more."

Up the river went the human king with his retinue until he came to the foot of the mango tree. There, swinging from branch to branch, the monkeys were chattering and eating the golden fruit. "The monkeys are eating my mangos." he cried. "They must be killed."

The king's archers surrounded the little monkeys and stood with their bows ready. Shivering with fright, the little monkeys cried to the Monkey King, "What can we do?"

"Have no fear!" said the Monkey King, and he tied his feet to a branch with a vine. Stretching out his long body, he sprang into the air, making a bridge from the tree to the far bank of the river. "Come monkeys, run across my back," he called. And the 80,000, monkeys ran across his back to safety on the other side.

The King of Benares, seeing all that was done, said to the archers, "It's not right that this Monkey King should die. Put away your bows and arrows and help him down from the tree."

As soon as the Monkey King's feet touched the ground, the King of Benares bowed to him, saying, "Great is a king who is willing to sacrifice his own life for his subjects. I have learned a valuable lesson from you today."

Forgetting about the mangos, the King of Benares returned to his palace and ruled kindly and wisely for the rest of his life. And the 80,000 monkeys returned to the mango tree round like the moon. They jumped from branch to branch, chattering and eating the golden fruit that was big and sweet and delicious.

Forgetting about the mangos, the King of Benares returned to his palace and ruled kindly and wisely for the rest of his life.

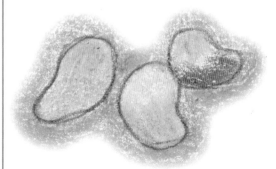

The Wounded Swan

When the Buddha was a young prince named Siddhartha, he often played with his cousin, Devadatta. One day they were practicing archery by the royal lake, shooting at stumps. Suddenly they heard the cry of a swan flying up from the lake. Lowering their bows, they watched the great white bird soar gracefully into the clear blue sky, heading for the distant peaks of the Himalayan Mountains.

Without warning, Devadatta quickly drew his bow and let the arrow fly. Zippp!

"Don't shoot, Devadatta!" Siddhartha cried. But it was too late. With a sharp cry, the swan tumbled down from the sky and fell to the ground.

Siddhartha ran as fast as he could to the swan. "I must save it." With his soft hand, he gently stroked the trembling swan as he pulled the sharp arrow out of its wing.

Devadatta came running up, shouting, "You stole my bird! It's mine. I shot it."

"I'll never give it to you. You'll only kill it." said Siddhartha. "Animals love their lives as much as people do. And they also have families. Who will take care of the baby swans if the mother dies? Let us go to the palace and ask the wise sages to decide who should get the bird."

At the palace, the wise sages heard each prince tell his side of the story. One sage said, "The swan belongs to Devadatta. After all, he shot it."

Another said, "Prince Siddhartha found it. So it should go to him."

Then the youngest sage said, "The swan should go to the one who will save its life, not to the one who will destroy it." The others agreed, and the swan was given to Siddhartha.

For the next few days Siddhartha cared for the swan until it could fly again. Taking it to the lake, he turned it loose so it could live freely with its own kind. "Fly far, far away so you will be safe." he said. And the swan flew high into the bright morning sky.

Hiding behind a tree, Devadatta watched the swan disappear. "I'll get even with Siddhartha one day," he said.

From then on, he teased Siddhartha and called him a coward, but Siddhartha did not mind. "Devadatta is still my friend," he said.

"Animals love their lives as much as people do. And they also have families. Who will take care of the baby swans if the mother dies?..."

The Kind Elephant Calf

Ages ago in the foothills of the Himalaya Mountains, the Buddha was born as a magnificent elephant calf. He was strong and brave and as white as a lotus flower. His mother called him Sati.

Sati followed his mother everywhere. She gave him sweet mangos and bathed him in sparkling pools of water, among the fragrant lotuses. In the hot afternoons, she rested in the shade of the blooming sala trees while he romped with the other elephant calves.

Over the years, Sati grew bigger and stronger and his mother grew older and weaker. In time, she lost her sight. Sati gave her the sweetest mangos and bathed her in sparkling pools. Then he guided her to rest in the shade of her favorite sala tree while he roamed with his friends.

One day the King of Kashi saw Sati, who had grown by now into a huge white elephant. "What a splendid animal to ride upon in my royal howdah!" he said.

And so the king captured Sati and put him in the royal stables. There he adorned him with silk and jewels and flower garlands. He gave him sweet grass and offered him water from his very own hand. But Sati would not eat or drink. He wept and wept, growing thinner and thinner each day.

"Noble elephant," said the king, "I adorn you with silk and jewels. I give you the sweetest grass and purest water, yet you do not eat or drink. What will please you?"

Sati said, "Silk and jewels, food and drink do not make me happy. My old mother is sightless and alone in the forest with no one to care for her. Even though I die here, I shall take neither food nor water until I give her some first."

Tears came to the king's eyes. "Never have I seen such filiality to one's parents, not even among humans," he said. "It is wrong to keep you in chains."

At the King's command, Sati was led to the sala grove and set free. Through the hills he raced, searching for his mother. He found her by a lotus pool. There she lay in the mud, too weak to move. Filling his trunk with water, he gave her drink and sprayed the top of her head and back until she shone.

"Is it raining?" she asked. "Or has my son returned to me?"

"It is your very own son!" he cried, "The king has set me free."

His mother said, "May the King of Kashi and his queen rejoice today as I rejoice at having my son back."

Sati plucked the sweetest mangos from a tree and gave them to her. He told her how he was captured, taken to the royal stables and was offered silk and jewels. But most of all, he told her of the king's kindness in setting him free to care for her again.

"Silk and jewels, food and drink do not make me happy. My old mother is sightless and alone in the forest with no one to care for her..."

Buddha, the Doctor

Once upon a time in a quiet monastery near the holy city of Benares there was a young monk named Tisha. He wore a yellow robe and lived the simple secluded life of a monk. Every morning he walked to the village with the other monks to collect offerings of food. After carrying water and sweeping the paths in the afternoons, he sat in quiet meditation. And in the evenings he recited prayers for a peaceful world.

One day he fell sick. His body broke out in sores and oozed with pus. Miserable and weak with fever, he lay in bed, groaning day and night. When the other monks saw him, they looked away in disgust. "He's hopeless," they said and left him alone.

At that time, the Buddha happened to visit the monastery with his faithful attendant, Ananda. He went from hut to hut, inspecting each one to see if the monks kept them clean.

Outside Tisha's hut, the Buddha heard a low moan. Upon opening the door, he saw Tisha lying in his own filth. "Boil some water over a fire and make a wash with *neem* leaves," he said to Ananda. "Then bring it to me."

When the water was ready, the Buddha gently washed Tisha's sores with his own hands. Ananda washed his soiled clothes and dried them. Then the Buddha and Ananda lifted him onto a clean bed and gave him warm broth to drink.

Tisha opened his eyes and gazed at the Buddha. "If you had not helped me, I would have died," he said.

The Buddha rubbed Tisha on the crown of his head. "Abide in peace," he said and quietly left the hut.

When the monks saw the Buddha caring so tenderly for Tisha, they bowed their heads in shame. "Tisha is our friend," they said. "We should have been more patient and helped him. After all, we are monks."

Comfort them, the Buddha raised his golden arm and said, "O monks! Your fathers and mothers are not here to take care of you. If you do not help each other, who will do so? Helping others is the same as serving the Buddha."

Upon hearing these words, the monks bowed in gratitude to the Buddha for his teaching of patience and compassion.

"If you do not help each other, who will do so? Helping others is the same as serving the Buddha."

The Buddha and the Dragon

Old Kasyapa, the most famous fire worshipper in Uruvilva, was known for his spiritual powers. He could walk on a bed of hot coals and swallow fireballs without getting burned. Every full moon he made sacrifices of fat sheep to the fire god.

When the Buddha heard about him, he said, "I must stop this useless killing of animals." But to talk to Old Kasyapa would be in vain. So he made a plan.

One rainy night he passed by Old Kasyapa's hut and asked, "May I stay here tonight? I can go no further."

Not knowing who the Buddha was, Old Kasyapa said, "You're welcome to stay in the cookhouse." But he did not tell the Buddha about his pet dragon.

Inside the cookhouse, the Buddha spread some grass on the floor and sat in meditation. Around midnight, a fierce looking dragon stuck its nose in the door and said, "Oh, a guest! It's a good thing I'm hungry."

The dragon was huge. It was horrible. It was scary and lime green. It took a deep breath and spit a huge ball of fire at the Buddha. Shish! But the Buddha was not afraid. He concentrated on loving-kindness and could not be burned.

"Now look," the dragon said, "I don't like this. Everyone else is afraid of me. As soon as I look at them, they run away screaming."

"Why should I be afraid of you?" said the Buddha. "You're just a miserable old dragon who treats others badly. If you were kind, you would be happy and have a world of friends."

"It's true," said the dragon, tears streaming down his scaly cheeks. "All I do is scare people. I don't know how to be kind."

"Then I'll teach you," said the Buddha. "Come, get into my begging bowl." And to the dragon's surprise, the Buddha shrank him into a tiny dragon about the size of a thimble. At once happy, the little dragon clambered into the bowl. Curling up inside, he went fast asleep.

The next morning Old Kasyapa opened the door of the cookhouse, expecting to find his guest burned to ashes. "Here's your dragon!" said the Buddha, holding out his bowl. Out climbed the happy little dragon, shining like a jewel in the bright morning light.

"If I become your disciple, will you teach me to do that?" asked Old Kasyapa.

"I don't know. My disciples don't sacrifice animals. They concentrate on loving-kindness. Can you?"

"Yes, I can," said Old Kasyapa. "Now I understand the true meaning of power." At these words, he threw his sacrificial tools into the river and became a devoted disciple of the Buddha. And the little dragon returned to his home in the river bottom where the dragons live.

"...If you were kind, you'd be happy and have a world of friends."

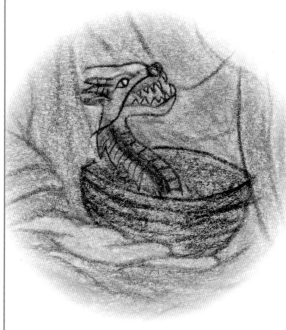

21

Old Birdsnest

Once upon a time in India there lived an old king who wanted to study the wisdom of the Buddha. Traveling throughout his kingdom, he searched for wise advisors and sages who could satisfy his longing. He visited famous teachers and great scholars of learning. He sought out hermits in dark mountain caves. For hours and hours he listened to them give long-winded explanations. In the end, he learned nothing about the wisdom of the Buddha.

"There is a wise old sage who lives in a bird's nest. Go ask him," a traveler told the king.

So the king set out immediately to find the wise sage. He followed a winding path high into the mountains until he came to a cherry tree in full bloom. Upon the highest branch sat an old sage in a huge bird's nest. Peeping up into the tree, the king called out, "Old Birdsnest, I am the king of Kosala and have a most important question to ask you."

The king waited for a greeting, but only heard the quiet sound of bees buzzing among the cherry blossoms. Annoyed, the king went on, "Well, this is the question. What is the most imporatnt teaching of the Buddha?"

There was a long silence—just the soft buzz of the bees. Finally the sage called down, "Don't harm anyone and do only good. Have a pure heart."

"What a foolish thing to say," said the king. "You're supposed to be a wise sage. I traveled all this way to find you. Is this all you can come up with? Why, even a three-year-old child could say that."

"True, a three-year-old could say it," said Old Birdsnest. "But it is difficult to do, even for an old man like me."

The old king smiled and nodded his head.

"Don't harm anyone and do only good. Have a pure heart."

Aryatara Kandahsari

Cintya Kandahsari

Aryatara and Cintya Kandahsari are sisters from the island of Jawa in Indonesia.

In 1995, they traveled with their parents all the way from a small town outside of Jakarta to another small town, Ukiah, California, to begin life as second and fifth graders at Instilling Goodness Elementary School at the City of Ten Thousand Buddhas.

Soon, the two young girls set to work illustrating the teachings of the Buddha, using oil pastels, graphite pencil and color pencil.

Bibliography

Below is a list of books that were used as sources and background.

A Treasury of Wise Action. Berkeley: Dharma Publishing, 1993.

Cowell, E.B., ed. *The Jataka or Stories of the Buddha's Former Births.*
Translated from the Pali. London: Pali Text Society, 1999;
Distributed by Motilal Banarsidass, Delhi.

Hsuan Hua, Venerable Master, *Talks on Dharma.*
Burlingame, CA: Buddhist Text Translation Society, 1984.

Buddhist Studies. Singapore:
Curriculum Development Institute of Singapore, 1984.

The Dharma Realm Buddhist Association

The Dharma Realm Buddhist Association (DRBA) was founded by the Venerable Master Hsuan Hua in the United States of America in 1959 to bring the genuine teachings of the Buddha to the entire world. Its goals are to propagate the Proper Dharma, to translate the Mahayana Buddhist scriptures into the world's languages and to promote ethical education. The members of the Association guide themselves with six ideals established by the Venerable Master which are: no fighting, no greed, no seeking, no selfishness, no pursuing personal advantage, and no lying. They hold in mind the credo:

Freezing, we do not scheme.

Starving, we do not beg.

Dying of poverty, we ask for nothing.

According with conditions, we do not change.

Not changing, we accord with conditions.

We adhere firmly to our three great principles.

We renounce our lives to do the Buddha's work.

We take responsibility in molding our own destinies.

We rectify our lives to fulfill our role as members of the Sangha.

Encountering specific matters, we understand the principles.

Understanding the principles, we apply them in specific matters.

We carry on the single pulse of the patriarchs' mind-transmission.

During the decades that followed DRBA's establishment, international Buddhist communities such as Gold Mountain Monastery, the City of Ten Thousand Buddhas, the City of the Dharma Realm, and various other branch facilities were founded. All these operate under the traditions of the Venerable Master and through the auspices of the Dharma Realm Buddhist Association. Following the Buddhas' guidelines, the Sangha members in these monastic facilities maintain the practices of taking only one meal a day and of always wearing their precept sashes. Reciting the Buddha's name, studying the teachings, and practicing meditation, they dwell together in harmony and personally put into practice Shakyamuni Buddha's teachings. Reflecting Master Hua's emphasis on translation and education, the Association also sponsors an International Translation Institute, vocational training programs for Sangha and laity, Dharma Realm Buddhist University, and elementary and secondary schools.

The Way-places of this Association are open to sincere individuals of all races, religions, and nationalities. Everyone who is willing to put forth his or her best effort in nurturing humaneness, righteousness, merit, and virtue in order to understand the mind and see the nature is welcome to join in the study and practice.